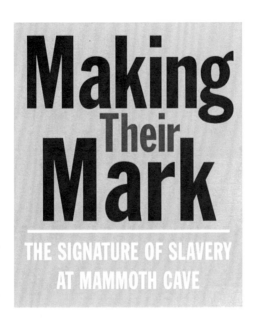

Making Their Mark

THE SIGNATURE OF SLAVERY AT MAMMOTH CAVE

BY

JOY MEDLEY LYONS

Eastern National

Serving the Visitors to America's
National Parks and Other Public Trusts

EASTERN NATIONAL • FORT WASHINGTON, PENNSYLVANIA

Published by Eastern National, Fort Washington, Pennsylvania
© 2006 Joy Medley Lyons   Reprinted 2022

Eastern National promotes the public's understanding and support of
America's national parks and other public trust partners by providing
quality educational experiences, products, and services.
Visit us at ShopANP.com
ISBN 1-59091-037-0

Cover Photo:
In 1863, Mammoth Cave explorer Ed Hawkins was born a slave at Glasgow Junction, nine
miles from the entrance to Mammoth Cave. He spent all his life within a 10-mile radius of
the cave until illness took him to Western State Hospital in Hopkinsville, Kentucky during
his final five years. Hawkins died in 1936 and is buried in the hospital cemetery, nearly 100
miles from home.

Photo Credit:
Neville photo from the Cave Research Foundation Collection. Special thanks to
Roger McClure and Gary Berdeaux.

IN MEMORY...

Of all whose heritage was muddled or lost as they sacrificed home and community for "the greater good" and Mammoth Cave National Park. Thank you for your priceless gift.

For my daughters, Rebekah and Hayley, who choose to judge people not "by the color of their skin, but by the content of their character." I love you.

Preface

I met David Bransford in the early 1990s. He was kind enough to let me and fellow researcher and friend Jeanne Schmitzer interview him at his home in Glasgow, Kentucky. David grew up on Flint Ridge near Mammoth Cave prior to the establishment of the national park, and was nearly 80 years old. He was an expressive man with a wonderful memory, a quick wit, a powerful voice and eyes that met ours straight on. Every moment spent with him brought us closer to the people we sought—his people.

David was the great-grandson of Materson Bransford, better known as "Mat," one of the first black guides at Mammoth Cave. Mat was brought to the cave as a slave in 1838. The Bransford legacy at Mammoth Cave began with this young slave guide, not yet out of his teens. Through three generations Mat's unbroken legacy continued until 1939, with the retirement of Mat's grandson Louis.

Along with slaves Stephen Bishop and Nicholas "Nick" Bransford, Mat explored previously unknown passages, guiding lantern-wielding travelers through the underground labyrinth. Mat led tours for 50 years. Mat's son, Henry, learned the routes and guided tours as his father's peer. Three of Henry's four sons and numerous grandsons continued the Bransford legacy underground. Grandson Louis, the last of the Bransford guides at Mammoth Cave, remained on the guide rolls until his 1939 retirement.

The third and fourth generation of Mammoth Cave Bransfords sold their homes to fellow Kentuckians committed to protecting the cave region and promoting tourism. In 1941, thanks to an act of Congress, Mammoth Cave National Park was created.

It was the 1970s before another black man led visitors through Mammoth Cave. This time he was not a slave or freed slave, he wore the green and gray uniform of a National Park Service seasonal employee.

My interview with David Bransford opened the door to his family, including sons Jerry, Michael, Larry and David, Jr. I was hoping to find lost pieces of Mammoth Cave's history, including their family's guiding history. Instead, I found myself sharing Mammoth Cave stories they had never heard. During my conversations with David's son, Jerry, I was surprised when the most basic elements I mentioned about their Mammoth Cave legacy seemed new to him. The history Jerry knew was that of his father's generation and did not include earlier ancestors. I became committed to giving the descendants of Mat Bransford their past—not just for their own sense of place and family, but out of respect for the men whose lives and deaths at Mammoth Cave now meant so much to me.

Jerry Bransford and I began a friendship that continues to this day. During the course of the friendship, we talked about the men in his family and their years as Mammoth Cave guides. We talked about the challenges of raising children in rural Kentucky and the fact that guiding tours at Mammoth Cave was seasonal work, especially in the earliest days of tourism in cave country.

One especially memorable story Jerry shared was a tale from his childhood. His father, David, was born within a couple of miles of Mammoth Cave. David was in grade school when his father, John Henry, sold their farm and moved the family from Edmonson to Barren County. Through the years, David maintained his connection to Mammoth Cave. He started bringing his own family to the cave when they were small and told them about the farm on which he lived, his neighbors, the segregated school he attended and the extended family of Bransfords that had lived within walking distance for several generations. He talked to them about the Bransford guides—how they came to the cave as slaves and found new cave passages, while working side-by-side with white men. He told them about how they lived next door to white families and bought and sold land from and to white men. And he told them about how children went to a segregated school, but when the school day was over, they played with white children who lived on small farms scattered along the remote country roads.

David also told his boys about the old hotel that burned down just before he was born and about the "new" old hotel that was built to take its place in the '20s. He told them about the little train, with its one engine and passenger car that sputtered up and down along the nine-mile track that stretched from Glasgow Junction to Mammoth Cave, dropping off cave visitors, and then struggling its way back. David made the journey from the cave to Glasgow Junction several times as a child.

The car trips David Bransford took with his boys to Mammoth Cave National Park were not as exciting as a train ride, but the family always looked forward to a special ice cream treat once they got there. After peering into the twilight of Mammoth Cave's locked entrance gate, David would follow the Old Guides' Trail up the ravine from the cave entrance where refreshing cool cave air mingled with the summer heat. He would wind his way toward the frame hotel perched on the sandstone at the top of the ridge, brushing away tree limbs and slowing his pace to keep his sons together behind him. Up the hill they would climb, away from the beckoning breath of the cave, beneath the shade of tulip poplars, sycamores and oaks and then out into the full sunlight of the freshly mowed hotel lawn.

Then David would lead his young family toward the walkway that welcomed thousands to the hotel's main entrance, occasionally placing a foot on the very same spot where his great-grandfather, Mat, had stepped.

The surfaced path branched away from the covered front portico, and David turned with it. Jerry Bransford would follow his father to the back door of the hotel where ice cream was sold to them. It was the 1950s and he and his brothers all knew their father's money was not welcome at the front. They ate the cold, sweet ice cream sitting at the back stoop of the Mammoth Cave Hotel, out of sight of the main traffic flow.

I went with Jerry out into the heart of the Mammoth Cave forest one autumn day, in search of the small cemetery where his ancestors were buried. I enlisted the help of friend and coworker Henry Holman, who was more familiar with the wooded area than I. We drove to Great Onyx Cave Road, where our hike began. Laying a map across the hood of the car, Henry took a quick compass bearing and then headed off into the woods. A hand motion signaled that Jerry and I should follow.

We didn't even try to keep up with Henry's fast pace. I was content to keep him within whistling distance as Jerry and I plodded through a mixture of cedars, pines and hardwoods. We closed the gap only when Henry stopped near a small cedar grove. He was standing still and gazing toward the ground.

Jerry and I stepped over small fallen trees and moved to stand with our trailblazer. Homes with orchards and a cool spring, hillside pastures and tilled crops had once been here. They were gone now, and the only sounds remaining were those from the woods around us.

Numerous upright limestone slabs thrust upward from fallen leaves on the forest floor, hinting of other graves and lost family. But we were here to look at only two of them. For the first time in his memory, Jerry gazed down upon the graves of his paternal great-grandparents.

The pair of stones before us bore the names of Alice Bransford, a beloved wife and mother, and her husband, Henry Bransford. Henry had been Alice's spouse for more than two decades. He fathered their six children, and not all were quite grown when he died. He had timbered wood before walking the few miles up the ridge to his guiding job at Mammoth Cave, only to walk back in the early evening and work crops long after dark by lantern light. He worked so hard and so long that a heart attack took him from his family when he was only 45 years old.

Henry's carefully etched stone had been purchased by Alice and their children and placed there to honor his memory. The inscription they selected described their husband and father in what they must have believed to be the most loving and definitive way:

"Henry Bransford, Guide"

With but three words is the sum of a man's life remembered.

A Cave in the West

T he American colonists had not yet won their independence when Englishmen such as Dr. Thomas Walker and Colonel Christopher Gist began to push the boundary of Virginia west in 1750. Coming through the Cumberland Gap must have been similar to "pushing" a newly discovered cave passage to see how far it goes and how many leads it has in various directions.

The gap through the Cumberland Mountains was used before by others. First, generations of herds of bison pounded through it, creating an obvious route that was close to reliable water sources. Then, American Indians moved east to west and back again as they hunted game in their nomadic and seasonal way.

After the French and Indian War, the English were eager to try their luck at establishing new settlements in and beyond the mountains. By 1776, many colonists were interested in escaping taxation and other perceived perils of the colonies. Men looked toward the expansive west of a continent whose boundaries had yet to be defined. They risked their lives and all their possessions and followed men like John Finley and Daniel Boone into the western interior. They fought alongside family and slaves to forge new settlements at Harrodstown and Boonesborough in what was soon called Fincastle County, Virginia. In June 1792, this American West became the 15th state of the Union and Virginia's western-most county became Kentucky, a pro-slavery state.

Following the American Revolution, the new nation awarded its war veterans with land grants in the West, and made other parcels available for purchase. Surveyors Richard Anderson, William Croghan (pronounced Kron) and others spent months traveling by river and horseback in the 1780s, establishing surveys and documenting natural resources along the way. Only four years before Meriwether Lewis and William Clark began their famed Corps of Discovery journey into the continent's interior in 1803, one of these land grants along the south side of Kentucky's Green River was awarded to young Valentine Simons. His surveyed deed describes the 200 acres he accepted as including "two saltpetre caves."[1] According to Cecil Goode, in his book *World Wonder Saved:* "At this early time, the caves had no particular value or use—merely a curiosity—

and the land of the area was the least desirable, being rough and rocky ridge land; but it was cheap, as a grant from the state could be obtained for as little as $40 for a hundred acres and could be used for subsistence farming. This was the time when the new settlers craved land, even poor land. After all, that was why they came over the mountains to Kentucky in the first place."[2]

Gunpowder was an immediate necessity for the earliest Europeans in Kentucky, who found themselves more than 400 miles from established settlements and retail sources in Virginia. Many historians credit Monk Estill, a former slave who was granted freedom due to bravery he exhibited during an American Indian raid, as the first man to manufacture gunpowder west of the Appalachians. Estill learned how to process gunpowder in Virginia. Settlers mined saltpeter from local rock shelters and men like Monk Estill mixed the saltpeter with just the right amounts of charcoal and sulphur to make gunpowder, knowing the survival of the settlements depended upon it.[3]

While mining saltpeter from rock shelters for local use could be accomplished by a small group of settlers or even one farmer, mining saltpeter in a cave could be a full-time endeavor. Such was the case with Mammoth Cave. The story has long been told at Mammoth Cave that saltpeter extracted from the rich soil inside the cave helped the United States avoid defeat in the War of 1812. That oral tradition has been neither proven nor disproven, but it is highly unlikely that Mammoth Cave saltpeter was combined with charcoal and sulphur to make all the gunpowder used in that war.

Before Mammoth Cave was even named, it was likely a source of saltpeter for its earliest owners. Valentine Simons did not hold his 200-acre land grant on the Green River for long. Within a few short years, he sold the land to John Flatt for $116.67. Flatt kept the tract for a few years before selling to the McLean brothers—George, Leonard and John, of Hart County, for $400.

Those earliest owners probably utilized the saltpeter resources of "Flatt's Cave" for their own needs and the needs of their neighbors. When the McLeans sold 156 acres of the property to Fleming Gatewood of Louisville and Charles Wilkins of Lexington, however, saltpeter extraction in the two caves became a major production. And the first period of profit speculation began at what was soon promoted as "Mammoth Cave" by Gatewood and Wilkins.

By 1804, most of the northern states had abolished slavery (all of colonial America participated in slavery, even after the Revolutionary War). In spite of that, businesses in states bordering Kentucky, like Indiana and Ohio, often leased slaves from their Kentucky owners to work as laborers in salt mines and similar industries.

Oral tradition has long maintained that as many as 70 slaves were leased to work inside Mammoth Cave, producing saltpeter from the natural cave sediments. This number has never been validated. One-room log cabins were constructed to house the slaves. Many years later, these cabins were clapboarded and put under one roof to form a row of rooms and a covered promenade on the first Mammoth Cave Hotel.

Seventy slaves are a lot of people, even if they worked in shifts. Crops would have been cultivated and harvested for their sustenance. They may have hunted or trapped game or fished in Green River. It would have been necessary to bring in staple goods, clothing, some tools and other supplies from Bowling Green or Louisville. There were slave owners in Warren, Barren, Hart and Edmonson Counties, and certainly they did not have steady work for a large group of slaves throughout the year. The collective source of manpower for the saltpeter enterprise remains unknown. As a matter of record, 75 percent of the slave owners in Kentucky owned only one slave in 1810. Another 20 percent owned fewer than five, leaving only five percent of the owners maintaining more than five slaves each. Those who owned multiple slaves were well-propertied families who farmed bottomland along Kentucky's rivers or managed large estates in the bluegrass interior.

One Mammoth Cave park ranger shared a story with me of meeting a man near Bowling Green, Kentucky, who told him that his family had supplied slaves for the nitrate works at the cave. The park ranger, who was at once intrigued, asked the gentleman how many slaves his family had leased to Mammoth Cave, and the fellow replied that he was told it was 70. Excited now, the ranger asked if he had family papers documenting the fact. At this the fellow smiled and replied, "No, I have something better. I heard it on a tour at Mammoth Cave."

At any rate, there were thousands of pounds of saltpeter produced from Mammoth Cave and a lot of men worked hard to produce it. The owners continued the operation until doing so was no longer profitable. There may be some small truth to the idea that Mammoth Cave helped win the War of 1812. But the bigger truth is that Mr. Eleuthere I. DuPont, a gunpowder manufacturer in Wilmington, Delaware, was able to widely distribute the gunpowder produced from Mammoth Cave saltpeter. And, due to political maneuvers by England, gunpowder was not being imported from abroad. There were enough people in the United States needing gunpowder in their daily lives at home to make operations like the one at Mammoth Cave lucrative.

By 1812, the Mammoth Cave production had already decreased due to natural intervention. A series of earthquakes centered in New Madrid, Missouri occurred in 1811 and 1812 and caused damage to the wooden vats, pipelines and pump tower timbers inside the cave. The earthquakes frightened the underground workers and overseers so much that no one was eager to enter the cave again for months. When the War of 1812 began, Mammoth Cave nitrate production was still profitable, but declining. In 1815, the operation discontinued altogether and the leased slaves returned to their owners. It wasn't until 1820, five years after the end of the war, that the first commercial coal mine, the "McLean Drift Bank," began production in Kentucky near the Green River and a community called Paradise in Muhlenburg County.

At least two pieces of documentation have come to light concerning slaves leased at Mammoth Cave during the final years of saltpeter production. A letter dated June 24, 1815, written by William Bell (Fleming Gatewood's brother-in-law) to John Hendrick, bears the names and values of 13 slaves. One of those listed is described as "Tambo." A second letter, from cave overseer Archibald Miller to John Hendrick in January of 1814, reads:

> DEAR SIR:
>
> YOUR BOY TAMBO IS VERY SICK AND I WISH YOU TO COME OVER AND SEE HIM. I WAS EXPECTING YOU ON ~~SUNDAY~~ MUNDAY LAST. I HAVE BLED HIM TWICE AND WILL GIVE HIM A SWETT TO DAY. I HAVE GOT NO MEDICAN AT PRESENT. I WISH YOU TO COME AND SEE HIM AND COME AS SOON AS YOU CAN.
>
> RESPECTFULLY
> A MILLER[4]

Fleming Gatewood married Elizabeth Slaughter of Mercer County in December 1811, shortly after the first earthquake hit.[5] Sometime in 1812, Gatewood sold his half interest in the partnership to Hyman Gratz of Pennsylvania, but retained some surface acreage nearby. The Gatewoods then moved to another part of Warren County. This left Irish immigrant Archibald Miller and his family to serve as caretakers of Mammoth Cave and the Gratz holdings. Miller had been working at the cave for about five years and for the next two decades Miller and his son, Archibald, Jr., escorted travelers adventuring through the American West into the few known miles of cave. Around 1832, Gatewood returned to Mammoth Cave where he and his sons, 16-year-old George Slaughter and 14-year-old E. B., led tours when needed. In 1835, the family left Mammoth Cave for good.[6]

Following Fleming Gatewood's departure, his nephew, Robert Slaughter Bell, and neighbor Robinson Shackleford and his son, Joseph, joined the Millers as Mammoth Cave guides. During the first 22 years of tourism in this wild western region, a handful of guides showcased the cave, and they were all Caucasian.

*O*ne evening in 1992, I accompanied a group of National Park Service employees into the natural entrance of Mammoth Cave. Hiking about one-half mile into the cave, we crossed the metal bridge spanning Bottomless Pit, a 105-foot-deep chasm, and climbed downward into a narrow, winding passage leading to another called the Labyrinth. Moving single file, the old trail illuminated by lanterns and hard hats with headlamps, the group climbed up and over rocks that had long since broken from the ceiling, safely straddling one dark crevasse, then spotting each other as we made a short jump over another. The journey terminated in a lower vestibule where the sandy floor seemed to spill in several directions—into one crawlway here, and another there. Each caver explored the room alone, enjoying the feeling of solitary discovery, knowing it was only a matter of minutes before our voices collided and filled the chamber with excited observations of the cave. On one wall was a charcoal drawing of a cannon and flag, sketched more than 150 years ago. Inscribed on another sand-colored patch of wall were four names. They were also dated. People stood on this very spot in 1838! The names, "Franklin Gorin," and "Robert Slaughter Bell," were each inscribed on the stone in what seemed to be their own hand. Beneath Bell's name is another name, that of his intended, "Maria Louisa Gorin." Had the lady ventured down here too? In skirts? And there, near her father's name—who is that, whose name was added by Gorin himself? Is this Stephen—Stephen Bishop? Our voices swelled together in excitement.

"BECAUSE THE ROAD WAS STEEP AND LONG,
AND THROUGH A DARK AND LONELY LAND,
GOD SET UPON MY LIPS A SONG
AND PUT A LANTERN IN MY HAND."

—JOYCE KILMER, 1886-1918
(FROM "LOVE'S LANTERN")

Follow Me. My Name is Stephen.

There is no person in Mammoth Cave history who is talked about more and understood less than Stephen Bishop. Despite years of research by various historians, his biographical information is almost non-existent until his arrival at Mammoth Cave in 1838. Mammoth Cave National Park officials have received hundreds of inquiries about him over the years. Authors of children's books want to write about his early life and later successes. Students write school reports about him. Reporters want to produce articles or films about him, with an emphasis on 19th-century race issues or cave exploration. All are challenged by gathering information on Stephen's early life as a slave. Facts and reminiscences of Stephen's childhood, like those of most slaves in American history, seem irretrievable.

In 1838, Hyman Gratz sold Mammoth Cave, nearby Dixon Cave and 1,300 surface acres to Franklin Gorin, an attorney whose family had helped settle the city of Glasgow in Barren County. Gorin had some personal interest in the cave property prior to the purchase. His daughter, Maria Louisa, married Robert Slaughter Bell. Robert and his father, William Bell, leased and operated a tavern nine miles south of the cave during the decade of the 1820s. By 1838, the Bells purchased the tavern and nearly 3,000 acres of land in Barren and Edmonson counties. Like Franklin Gorin, they were slave owners. Visitors to Mammoth Cave stopped at Bell's Tavern on their way to and from the famous landmark.

Immediately upon purchasing the cave property, Gorin began making improvements. He hired men to enlarge the existing house. He added a second story with a ballroom and more overnight lodging, a bigger dining room and more main floor lodging. He also enclosed the former slave cabins. A long portico served as a promenade, which ran the full length of the rambling structure. Gorin was interested in expanding the known cave routes, as well as the hotel. He dispatched others to explore the cave, occasionally venturing underground himself.

Franklin Gorin conducted legal business for many of his neighbors in Glasgow, Kentucky. Among these clients was Lowry Bishop, from whom he may have purchased the young slave, Stephen. In 1837, Lowry Bishop legally transferred to Gorin the authority to sell and convey his personal estate.[7] It is known that Stephen was Gorin's property in 1838 when he bought Mammoth Cave. When Gorin decided to expand the known cave passages, he brought Stephen from Glasgow to do it. He also leased Materson "Mat" Bransford and Nicholas Bransford from the Bransford family (first Thomas Bransford, then his son, Thomas L. Bransford), prosperous farmers who were from Glasgow, Kentucky.

Early visitor accounts written about Stephen Bishop describe him as having been anywhere from 16 to 18 years of age when he arrived at the cave. By all accounts, Stephen Bishop was mulatto (biracial). No one knows who Stephen's father was, but he was most certainly a white man. In fact, if Stephen's mother was also mulatto, Stephen's biological heritage was more Caucasian than African. As a young man taken from family, friends and familiar surroundings, Stephen must have felt a little daunted by his new position and responsibilities.

It is hard to know why Franklin Gorin chose Stephen Bishop for the tasks of seeking new cave passages and extending tour routes. Barren, Warren, Hart and Edmonson counties are riddled with sinkholes and caves. It is very likely that Mammoth was not the first cave Stephen saw or entered. By all accounts, Stephen was a quick study and physically fit. As a successful attorney, Franklin Gorin must have been an intelligent and analytical man. He knew everyone of any notoriety in the area. Did he bring the young man to Mammoth Cave simply because Stephen was his slave and, as such, had to do what he was told? Did Stephen somehow warrant certain privileges? Had he worn out his welcome in Glasgow? Was he already a caver of some local renown? Did he *ask* Gorin to give him the opportunity? Whatever his reasons, Franklin Gorin selected Stephen as the person best suited for the cave. Or, maybe, he decided Mammoth Cave was best suited for Stephen.

Who was this man, Stephen, and what was Mammoth Cave to him? No one can imagine the feelings Stephen had when he went into the cave day-after-day, often alone. Those who enjoy the benefits of political freedom cannot understand what it is like to be enslaved to another.

Every trip Stephen took underground had to be one of preparation. The cave is an alien environment to humans. The darkness is very real and decisively complete. The cave's temperature is not constant, as has been claimed, but can be very cold near the entrance and rarely climbs above 60 degrees Fahrenheit anywhere else in the cave. In summer, the cave exhales cool air at the entrance and entering the cave environment is a relief from the heat. Upon exiting the cave, the change from cool temperatures to the heat and humidity of an August day can be overwhelming. In winter, the cave draws in cold air at the gaping entrance, pushing at your back, almost propelling you toward the first large room—the Rotunda, located at the end of the entrance passageway called the Narrows. Exiting the cave through the Narrows in January can be painful when the wind chill drops well below zero degrees Fahrenheit, freezing the skin of your face and drying the moisture from your eyes.

Stephen ventured underground with at least one open flame lantern, maybe more. He may have carried extra fuel, candles or matches,[8] a little food for sustenance and rags to protect his hands or knees. Moving through the rock and rubble of Mammoth Cave was often a slow process with very limited light. Along his way, Stephen passed many of the same landmarks visitors see today. He saw the mounds of spent saltpeter dirt in the Rotunda and the next room, the Church. He saw the wooden water pipes made of logs and the square boxes set down in the gaping trenches that marked the original floor of Valentine Simon's day. Stephen found bits and pieces of items cast away by slaves who worked the saltpeter dirt in Mammoth Cave more than 20 years earlier. Maybe there was a broken bucket here, a ragged and sweat-stained head scarf there. He saw shovel marks in the brown dirt edging the walls and footprints in the soft dirt of side passages—some imprinted by the soles of shoes, some outlining the shape of a calloused foot.

Stephen Bishop scraped his way over every known square yard of the cave, looking for leads into passageways that had not been suitable for the saltpeter venture. He crawled and twisted into tight spaces only to come to a solid wall or jumbled pile of rocks and have to back his way out the full length of the passage. He watched for yawning holes in the floor and listened for the staccato sounds of water dropping into the cave through domes, sliding down through layer after layer of bedrock and into the open void of a vertical shaft.

Stephen grew accustomed to the peculiar nature of the cave, perhaps feeling that the cave was becoming more accustomed to him. Did he explore by day? By night? Did he enter the cave after breakfast and not return to his bed until long after everyone else had eaten supper? Had he truly become a caver, a seeker of a still unknown subterranean wilderness? He most certainly spent days at a time seeing nothing but darkness as he trudged beneath the canopy of the forest, then darkness underground. The heartiest cavers are like this.

As Stephen became more comfortable with the cave, partly due to tutelage from experienced guides Archibald Miller, Jr. and Joe Shackleford, he began to lead visitors into areas long toured by the Millers and Gatewoods. Then, he became more comfortable leading visitors into those passageways known to the earliest human explorers of the cave. He showed off pieces of twined slippers, gourd bowls and primitive cane torches scattered in side passages.

With the help of fellow slaves and others, Stephen worked to improve existing trails. His directive was to expand the tour routes, and he did just that. Stephen secured his place in Mammoth Cave history when he and a visitor, Mr. Stevenson, crossed the Bottomless Pit—which had previously blocked all continuing exploration—in late 1838. From that day, Stephen made his way daily into new and nameless rooms and passageways. He crawled and climbed over rocks to make his way into areas known today as Pensico Avenue, Bunyan's Way and the Scotsman's Trap. He crawled through the soft soil of river sediments, scraping his way over jutting and broken limestone, to finally enter a room where he stood up straight and proclaimed the spot "Great Relief Hall." Further excavations, in an effort to open the crawl for tourists, led to the discovery of "Fat Man's Misery," a snug and winding water-carved trail still used on cave tours.

Stephen continued to explore beyond Great Relief Hall, listening for the steady drops of water he hoped would lead to an underground stream. He must have felt cold waves of surprise and a little fear when he heard the echoing roar of a waterfall in a large passage bearing off to his left. That dynamic proclamation of gallons of running water pouring into a churning pool led Stephen on a treacherous journey over slick mud banks and drop-offs punctuated by cold, black water. He found the life's blood of the cave, more than 30 stories beneath the surface of the earth—an underground stream that was soon called "Echo River."

So, he marveled at the Dead Sea, Charon's Cascade, Echo River, the River Styx and Lake Lethe. Did Stephen name his new discoveries, or did the Glasgow attorney, Franklin Gorin? Which of the two was more likely to be familiar with ancient mythology? It must have been a pleasure to name such magnificent, never-before-seen places. And, if Stephen knew nothing of mythology before this adventure through Mammoth Cave's wet and youngest passageways, he certainly became familiar with it from that point on.

This young man, a slave, became the first man ever to see eyeless and colorless river animals—small fish, crayfish and even tiny shrimp. He captured a living specimen and took it to the hotel to show his master and was congratulated for his progress.

Stephen pushed beyond the known and quiet meanders of Mammoth Cave, becoming more familiar with the not-so-quiet, temperamental, ever-changing dynamic waterways of the newest and deepest levels of darkness. Truth be told, it was a tremendous amount of work, but when he was in the cave, young Stephen Bishop was probably having a great time.

Stephen, Charlotte, Thomas and the Doctor

Franklin Gorin had been acquainted with Louisville physician John Croghan for some time, having handled several of the Croghan family's legal matters in the southern part of the state. In 1839, Franklin Gorin sold Mammoth Cave and more than 1,600 acres of surrounding land to Dr. Croghan for $10,000. This was $5,000 more than the price Gorin paid for the cave property one year earlier. Croghan's offer, however, included the purchase of slave guide Stephen Bishop.

John Croghan was born in 1790 in Louisville, Kentucky. He was the oldest child of William Croghan and Lucy Clark Croghan. William Croghan was a veteran of the Revolutionary War and an early Kentucky surveyor. John Croghan's uncle, George Rogers Clark, founded the city of Louisville in 1778. At about age 16, young John, along with his brothers and sisters saw the return of another uncle, William Clark. Partnering with his friend Meriwether Lewis, Clark had just completed their great journey to the continent's west coast. Many of the curiosities collected during the Corps of Discovery were exhibited in the upstairs ballroom of Locust Grove, the Croghan home.

An adventurous nature seems to have run in the family. John had a strong interest in earth sciences, especially geology. As a student at Transylvania University, his study choices were limited. If he entered professional life, the most popular choices were the military, teaching or the practice of law or medicine. Croghan opted to become a physician. Prior to purchasing Mammoth Cave, Croghan speculated in a Kentucky salt mine along the Cumberland River. He invested in other property as well, but let go of the Cumberland River property when workers inadvertently polluted the river when they hit a pocket of oil. Having no use for the slick, smelly ooze, the doctor was happy to get a good price and have that parcel of land, and the now oily section of river, off his hands. He decided to seek his fortune elsewhere.

When Doctor Croghan bought the Mammoth Cave property and Stephen Bishop, he set about continuing Gorin's improvements to the property, including an expansion of the toured cave. Croghan also continued leasing Materson "Mat" Bransford and Nicholas Bransford.

While the issue of slavery was heating up in the United States, the exploration of Mammoth Cave continued. In previous years, the known length of the cave's passageways had been exaggerated—eight miles, 14 miles, 25 miles, 100 miles. With Stephen and Mat pursuing new cave passageways on a regular basis, fact was beginning to catch up with fiction. In 1840, these Kentucky slaves were exploring the far reaches of Mammoth Cave, while enslaved Africans revolted on the Spanish ship, *Amistad*, off the coast of Cuba.

Stephen went on to cross cave rivers and discover more "virgin" labyrinths—Silliman's Avenue, the Pass of El Ghor, Snowball Room, Croghan Hall, the Maelstrom. With Stephen's discovery of Mammoth Dome, a vertical shaft more than 20 stories high, the cave's growing reputation seemed to know no bounds.

Oral tradition has it that Stephen Bishop met his wife Charlotte, a mulatto slave, during a visit to Locust Grove in Louisville in 1842. While there, Dr. John Croghan's brother, Colonel George Croghan, had Stephen draw from memory a map of the explored passageways in Mammoth Cave. The map was credited to the slave, Stephen, when published in the book, *Rambles in the Mammoth Cave During the Year 1844, by a Visitor.*[9]

Charlotte returned to Mammoth Cave with Stephen and bore him a son, Thomas, in 1843. During this time period, Stephen helped Dr. Croghan care for patients in a consumptive hospital that was set up in the cave for five months. Now called tuberculosis, consumption was a common malady in Stephen's day and usually resulted in death. Dr. Croghan sought a cure by convincing as many as 15 patients to spend the winter months living in small stone or wood cabins in the cave. He theorized that the constant temperature might cure his patients. Some of them stayed underground for the entire five months, but most did not. Several died during the treatment and the others showed no real signs of improvement. The medical treatment was abandoned.

Visitors to Mammoth Cave, especially those from abroad, were often as impressed by the black guides as they were by the cave. As was customary, many of these travelers kept journals and published them upon their return home. They wrote numerous descriptions of Stephen Bishop, hinting toward the atypical role placed on the slave guides underground: "Our guide modestly remembered that he was a slave, and after the repast under the weight of which he had toiled so far, he seated himself at a distance; but, remembering his merits and all the geology and history he had given us on the way, we voted him to the first table by an immediate and general remonstrance."[10]

Some visitors described his physical features: "Stephen, who has a share in all the principal explorations and discoveries, is almost as widely known as the Cave itself. He is a slight, graceful, and very handsome mulatto of about thirty-five years of age, with perfectly regular and clearly chiseled features, a keen, dark eye, and glossy hair and moustache. He is the model of a guide—quick, daring, enthusiastic, persevering, with a lively appreciation of the wonders he shows, and a degree of intelligence unusual for one of his class."[11]

Others wrote about his knowledge of the cave and science: "His vocation has brought him into contact with many intellectual and scientific men and as he has great quickness of perception and a prodigious memory, he has profited much by intercourse with superior minds. He can recollect everybody that ever visited the cave, and all the terms of geology and mineralogy are at his tongue's end."[12]

Still others wrote about his desire for freedom and at least one claimed that Stephen intended to leave the cave. "The remarkable Stephen is a slave … with more the physiognomy of a Spaniard—his masses of black hair curling—slightly and gracefully, and his long moustache giving quite the Castillian air…. He is middle size, but built for an athlete—with broad chest and shoulders, narrow hips, and legs slightly bowed, and he is famous for his dexterity and bodily strength which are very necessary to his vocation…. The cave is a wonder which draws good society, and Stephen shows that he is used to it. His intelligent face is assured and tranquil, and his manners particularly quiet—and he talks to charming ladies with the air of a man who is accustomed to their good will, and attentive listening. The dress of the renowned guide is adapted to dark places and rough work. He wears a chocolate-colored slouched hat. A green jacket and striped trousers, and evidently takes no thought to his appearance…. He is married. His wife is the pretty mulatto chambermaid of the hotel. He has one boy, takes a newspaper, studies geology, and means to go to Liberia as soon as he can buy his wife, child and self from his present master."[13]

It is interesting to note that while there are only two known primary sources who state that Stephen Bishop intended to take his family to Liberia, many historians chose to take up that flag and wave it as fact. There is no real proof that Stephen ever intended to leave Mammoth Cave. Yet, those who spouted admiration and glowing accounts of the man seemed more than ready to ship him and his family off to a far away colony for repatriated African slaves.

Prior to purchasing Mammoth Cave, Doctor Croghan lost several brothers to consumption. On January 11, 1849, he died of the disease at his Louisville farm. An inventory of John Croghan's slaves described and estimated the value of the small Bishop family. Stephen was described as being about 28 years old, mulatto, approximately five-feet-10-inches tall, with a scar on his forehead, valued at $600. Charlotte, age 26, is described as mulatto, about five-feet-two-inches tall, compactly built, valued at $450. Young Thomas is described as six years of age and valued at $100.

Croghan died after spending fewer than 10 years at Mammoth Cave, but his influence remained for decades afterward. By the terms of his last will and testament, each of his many slaves was to be freed seven years after his death. During those seven years, they were to prepare themselves for manumission by working and earning a wage. Croghan never married and had no direct heirs. The Mammoth Cave property was left in trust to his nieces and nephews, with trustees managing the cave until the last heir died. Then, it was to be auctioned.[14]

Stephen continued to guide visitors through Mammoth Cave, while awaiting his freedom. Visitors frequently requested Stephen as their guide, and he was almost always sent into the cave when special visitors arrived, like transcendentalist author Ralph Waldo Emerson or the Swedish opera singer Jenny Lind.

Stephen, Charlotte and Thomas were given their freedom in 1856. In October of that year, Stephen paid $140 to purchase 75 acres of land from a white neighbor named Martin Shackleford. By the end of the summer of 1857, Stephen was gone. He died from unknown causes at age 37.

Stephen was buried behind the Mammoth Cave Hotel in the same small cemetery where he had helped lay to rest the doctor's deceased consumptive patients in 1842 and 1843. For years, only a cedar tree marked his grave. Three decades later, Pittsburgh businessman James R. Mellon visited the cave and was touched by the stories he heard of Stephen Bishop. Mellon promised Charlotte, who still worked in the hotel dining room, that he would have a stone for Stephen's grave prepared and sent down to Kentucky. It took a few years, but Mellon kept his word, sending a stone that had originally been intended for a Union veteran of the Civil War. The soldier's name was removed and Stephen's was engraved in its place. Stephen is buried in the "Old Guide's Cemetery," on a ridge above the entrance to Mammoth Cave.

The 1860 Edmonson County Census lists Charlotte Bishop as head of household, with three young boys (not her sons) in the house. Sixteen-year-old Thomas is found on a farm a little further down the road and across the Hart County line, working as a laborer for friend and neighbor William "Scott" Miller, the son of the elder Archibald Miller. By the time the 1870 census is taken, Charlotte is married to Stephen's fellow guide, Nicholas Bransford, who was widowed and has two grown daughters.

Thomas Bishop never appears on another Edmonson County census. In the early 1860s, Nick mentions in a land document that Charlotte is a widow and her son, Thomas, is deceased. The cause of Thomas' death is unknown, although he appears to have died during the years of the Civil War.

Many years later, in a letter to Maryland physician W. Stump Forwood, former slave owner Franklin Gorin wrote: "…I placed a guide in the cave—the celebrated and great Stephen—and he aided in making the discoveries. He was the first person who ever crossed the Bottomless Pit…. We discovered all that part of the cave now known beyond that point. Stephen was a self-educated man; he had a fine genius, a great fund of wit and humor, and some little knowledge of Latin and Greek, and much knowledge of geology; but his great talent was a perfect knowledge of man…. I knew his father, who was a white man. I owned Stephen's mother and brother, but not until after both children were born. Stephen was certainly a very extraordinary boy and man."[15]

In spite of the rhetoric of visitors about dreams of freedom and Liberia, Bishop never left Mammoth Cave or its people. It took death to spirit Stephen away from his wife, their son and the cave that beckoned and breathed in the bedrock beneath their home. Total manumission of slaves was less than a decade away, and Charlotte's life at the Mammoth Cave estate continued without Stephen … without their son. But she had Nick, the quiet guide of Mammoth Cave.

Dr. John Croghan, owner of Mammoth Cave from 1839 until his death from consumption in 1849, was the eldest son of William Croghan, an Irish immigrant and land surveyor. Like his maternal uncle, George Rogers Clark, Doctor Croghan never married. He bequeathed Mammoth Cave to the children of his younger brothers and sisters. By order of his will, all the doctor's slaves were emancipated seven years after his death.

Credit: Historic Locust Grove, Inc.

Built in 1791, Locust Grove was the home of William and Lucy Croghan and all their children. It was on a visit here that slave guide Stephen Bishop drew from memory a map of the explored passageways of Mammoth Cave.

Photo Credit: Historic Locust Grove, Inc.

Students at the one-room segregated Mammoth Cave School pose with their teacher, circa 1914. Most of these students had family who worked in some capacity at the Mammoth Cave Hotel.

Photo Credit: National Park Service (Clifton Bransford Collection)

Union veteran William Garvin, his wife, Hannah, and their children pose at their home near Mammoth Cave, circa 1880.

Photo Credit: National Park Service

Interaction between slave guides and Mammoth Cave visitors resulted in numerous documented accounts describing black men of the Mammoth Cave community. With the exception of oral history and some court documents, comparatively little is known about the mothers, wives and daughters who lived and worked in the area. Here, Mrs. Lizzie Duff, Mrs. Belle Gardner and Miss Rhoda Woodson pose for a photograph on September 17, 1911.

Photo Credit: National Park Service (Clifton Bransford Collection)

Jim Brown, an unidentified hotel cook and cave explorer Ed Hawkins sit together outside the Mammoth Cave Hotel, circa 1920.

Photo Credit: National Park Service

Transportation from the Mammoth Cave Hotel to and from Green River and around the hotel grounds was provided in various forms. The oxen driver in this photo is most likely cave guide Henry Bransford, circa 1890.

Photo Credit: National Park Service

Materson "Mat" Bransford, as sketched by Danish artist Ferdinand Richardt during the summer of 1857. Mat was approximately 37 years old.

Credit: Courtesy of Frank and Justina Keller

This studio portrait of slave guide Mat Bransford (circa. 1863) obviously celebrates his cave guide occupation. He poses with a grease lantern, walking stick, Kentucky basket (used for carrying lunches and other small items) and a fuel container.

Photo Credit: The Filson Historical Society, Louisville, Kentucky (Pettus-Speiden Collection)

This rare photograph of a young Ed Bishop was taken shortly after he became a guide at Mammoth Cave. Jerry Bransford discovered the original photograph in a box of mementos belonging to his father, David Bransford, following the elder Bransford's death in 2003.

Photo Credit: Bransford Family Collection

An early photo of Will Bransford, grandson of cave guide Mat Bransford. Will was born in 1866 and began guiding visitors through Mammoth Cave in 1887. This photo may have been taken shortly after he began guiding tours, as his pant legs are too long and his grip on the torch stick in his right hand seems tentative. Note the flower in his lapel, probably picked from the ground at the base of the tree. Fellow guide Ed Bishop can be seen behind Bransford.

Photo Credit: National Park Service (Clifton Bransford Collection)

This image of Will Bransford depicts a man more comfortable with the tools of his trade. Note the more confident grip on the torch stick, the rolled pant legs and the more cavalier clothing.

Photo Credit: National Park Service

Cave guide Bob Lively poses at the entrance to Mammoth Cave in the early 1900s. Lively's home was purchased for the creation of Mammoth Cave National Park. He moved his family to Louisville, Kentucky, where his descendants still live today.

Photo Credit: National Park Service

Ed Bishop was born in April 1866. By age 14, he had moved out of his mother's home and was working as a farm laborer in Cave City, Kentucky. By 1886 he was a Mammoth Cave guide—an occupation he continued until 1917. When his 31 years at Mammoth Cave came to an end, his work history became varied, including both railroad and janitorial work.

Photo Credit: The author's personal collection

Mr. M.W. BRANSFORD
GUIDE OF 3ʳᵈ GENERATION
Prop. of Bransford's Resort
MAMMOTH CAVE KY

David Bransford gave the author this postcard in 1994. Matt Bransford and his wife, Zemmie, provided lodging and meals for black visitors who came to Mammoth Cave. These visitors were often servants accompanying their employers while traveling. In an early 1920s letter to cave manager Judge Albert C. Janin in Washington, D.C., Matt Bransford assured Janin he would never allow his "negro tours" to cross paths with Caucasian tours in the cave. (The original letter is in the Janin Collection at the Huntington Library in California.)

Photo Credit: The author's personal collection

This image, circa 1931, depicts the integrated guide force on the steps of the Guide House. Seated, from left to right: Will Bransford, Bob Lively, Matt Bransford, John "Mutch" Hunter, Schuyler Hunt (Caucasian) and Louis Bransford. Standing, from left to right: Elzie Bransford; Lester Coats, Leon Hunt, Lyman Cutliff and Lloyd Wilson (all Caucasian); George Bransford, Lester Carney (Caucasian), Clifton Bransford, Arthur Bransford; Young Hunt, Charlie Hunt and Leo Hunt (sons of Schuyler); Louis Brown and Cebert Wilson, Lloyd's father. Seniority seems to have been the requirement for winning a seat in the photo.

Photo Credit: National Park Service

Pictured are five of the six senior members of the 1931 Mammoth Cave Guide Force. From left to right: John "Mutch" Hunter, Bob Lively, Will Bransford, Matt Bransford and Schuyler Hunt. Lively retired not long after this photo was taken. He received a nominal monthly pension of $10 from the Mammoth Cave heirs, but retained it only while the estate remained in private ownership.

Photo Credit: National Park Service

There were four different Civilian Conservation Corps camps at Mammoth Cave in the 1930s. This photo depicts enrollees from the segregated Camp #4 along with Caucasian enrollees from at least one of the other three camps. The man holding the first wheelbarrow at left is James "Tubby" Skaggs who went on to work for the National Park Service. Directly behind Skaggs' left shoulder is Lyman Cutliff, cave guide. In 1935, while directing Camp #4 in a cave trail improvement project, Cutliff and coworker Grover Campbell discovered the remains of a prehistoric man who was accidentally crushed to death on a cave ledge more than 2,000 years earlier.

Photo Credit: National Park Service

Cave guide Ed Bishop poses with a tour group prior to entering Mammoth Cave, circa 1912.

Photo Credit: National Park Service

The third generation of Bransford guides at Mammoth Cave is represented here by a young Matt, who strikes a debonair pose. Photo circa 1915.

Photo Credit: National Park Service (Wise Family Collection)

Guide Bob Lively poses for his pre-tour photograph, date unknown.

Photo Credit: National Park Service

Ed Bishop and Bob Lively pose with their cave tour group in a rare winter scene. The date for this photograph is not known, but it was taken no more than a few years prior to December of 1916, when the Mammoth Cave Hotel was destroyed by fire.

Photo Credit: National Park Service

Louis Bransford (front left) poses at the natural entrance of Mammoth Cave with his tour group, circa 1920. Louis was the last of the Bransfords to leave the guide service, only two years prior to the 1941 establishment of Mammoth Cave National Park.

Photo Credit: National Park Service

Slave guide "Alfred" is mentioned in published accounts written by 19th-century Mammoth Cave visitors. A contemporary of Stephen Bishop and Mat and Nick Bransford, Alfred's signature is seen in some of the cave's oldest tour passages.

Photo Credit: National Park Service photo by Eric Frey

From 1838 to early 1857, Stephen Bishop was considered by many to be the premier guide of Mammoth Cave. Slaves Alfred and Mat were also frequently mentioned in travel articles. After Stephen's death in the summer of 1857, Nick seems to have guided more frequently, as attested to by this graffiti written on the wall by visitors in the Snowball Room.

Photo Credit: National Park Service photo by Charles J. DeCroix

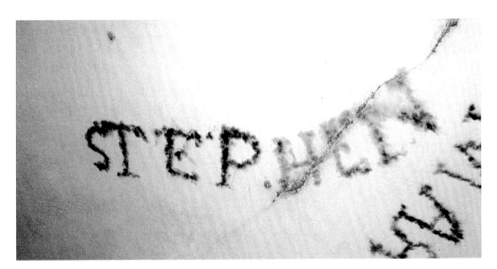

Guide Stephen Bishop's name is seen in dozens of areas inside Mammoth Cave. Visitors sometimes added their guide's name to the walls as if in tribute. Mammoth Cave explorers see Stephen's own signature in many places, both on and off tour trails. Interestingly, today's cavers are able to track Stephen's "penmanship" lessons by noting improvements made in his handwriting over time. Stephen usually wrote the year along with his signature, especially in newly discovered passageways.

Photo Credit: National Park Service photo by Charles J. DeCroix

Nicholas "Nick" Bransford was probably sitting on a comfortable rock just outside the entrance to Mammoth Cave when Richardt made this sketch. Although Nick was slightly older than Mat, Nick outlived his fellow guide by nearly 10 years.

Credit: National Park Service

While admiring original sketches drawn in 1857 by Danish artist Ferdinand Richardt, I gently picked up a fragile piece of yellowing sketch paper. The white cloth of the curatorial glove I wore stood stark against the 140-year-old drawing. The man in the sketch was identified as being Stephen Bishop according to park records. But, how likely was that? Stephen died during the summer the artist had visited Mammoth Cave. Would Stephen have looked so alive, so healthy, so ready to lead the artist underground? I studied the slight smile in his eyes, the hint of an upturn at his mouth, the full and tightly curled hair of an African slave. I thought of early photos I had seen of guides Nick and Mat Bransford. I remembered the well-worn slouch cap, the solid build, the craftsman's hands. "This isn't Stephen Bishop," I whispered to a nearby curator's case of prehistoric art, "This is Nick!"

To Nick, the Guide

Nicholas and Materson Bransford were taken to Mammoth Cave by Franklin Gorin at about the same time that Stephen Bishop was moved there. Early researchers and historians have reported that Mat and Nick were brothers. That is not the case. Visitor accounts describing Nick are hard to find. The lack of firsthand descriptions of Nick can lead to any of several conclusions. Because of his African appearance, Nick may have been the subject of preconceived ideas concerning slave intellect and bearing. Perhaps visitors were not as comfortable in his presence as they were with the mulatto guides. By most accounts, Nick was a plainspoken man, not the showman that Stephen was, and certainly not as literate. It could also be because Nick was not a regular guide while Stephen Bishop was still alive. It is possible that Stephen and Mat were able to handle most of the cave visitation between the two of them.

When Thomas Bransford died in 1853, both Nick and Mat became the property of his son, Thomas L. Bransford. According to documents filed in the Barren County Clerk's Office, the younger Bransford bought several slaves from his father's estate, and Mat and Nick were among them.[16]

After the elder Bransford's death, the inventory of his property listed Nick with a value of $800, substantially more than other slaves listed. It is possible that Nick Bransford was a tradesman, perhaps a skill he learned from his father. In a letter that Nick had a friend write to descendants of Thomas L. Bransford, Nick mentions his mother and father, "Joe," a blacksmith, coming to Kentucky from Virginia. Since Thomas Bransford came to Kentucky from Virginia, it is possible that Nick was born to Bransford slaves.[17]

Nick assisted with cave exploration, and he served as a tour guide, but he does not appear in traveler accounts until the years following Stephen Bishop's death in 1857. Oral tradition conveys that early slave guides learned to read and write while watching visitors carve or smoke their names on cave walls and ceilings. If this is the case, the lessons did not work for Nick or Mat, since legal documents filed in Edmonson County following their manumission bear their "mark" and not a signature.

Nick's dark skin may have caused him to have a little more trouble gaining compliance from the wealthy visitors he escorted underground. Certainly, his authoritative role as guide was atypical for slaves, or even freed slaves. As if to make the guide's job a little easier, a number of visitors offered words of wisdom to the elite who traveled underground. "One does what he (the guide) does and if he plunges head over heels into some dark chasm, then one imitates him cheerfully and believes confidently that he has a special point of interest up his sleeve."[18]

An 1897 guide manual, written 30 years after the slaves at Mammoth Cave were freed, warned: "The abrupt manner in which it is necessary for the guides to address visitors in dangerous places must not be confounded with insolence, as it is absolutely essential at many points."[19]

In 1867, a visitor wrote this about Nick: "In the evening, as I sat before the blazing pile of logs in the fireplace, someone knocked at my door and a Negro servant looked in. Would I like to see the guide? 'Certainly. What is his name?' 'Nicholas, sah, Nicholas! But we all calls him Ole Nick.' On presentation his Majesty proved to be an interesting black man, considerably past middle age; wrinkled, as none but a genuine Negro ever becomes: a short, broad strong man with a grizzled beard and moustache, quiet but steady eyes, grave in his demeanor, and concise in his conversation. He tells me of two routes by which I can make a tour through his domains."[20]

While Nick's less than flamboyant demeanor did not gain him the media coverage Stephen and Mat experienced, his style of guiding seemed to suit the visitor quoted above just fine. He wrote that Nick "seemed thoroughly imbued with the spirit of the place in which he had spent the greater portion of his time for 17 years. He was as grave and taciturn as some cave-keeping anchorite. During our inward progress, he had carefully pointed out every place and object of interest." The visitor went on to discuss the trip out of the cave, describing Nick as stalking ahead of him "silently and abstractedly," listening to every step of the visitor's feet. "If I paused or made a misstep, he instantly looked around."[21]

Englishman F. J. Stevenson visited Mammoth Cave in 1863 and spent much of his time underground with Nick. If one takes Mr. Stevenson's remembrances of that visit seriously, it is easy to see that Nick's regular assignment of escorting Mr. Stevenson may have elicited a less than enthusiastic response from the guide. The Englishman seems to have been a risk taker. The stoic and quiet Nick was *not*. "The light of my lamps was swallowed up in darkness and I could not make out neither roof, floor nor sides, until Nick made a sudden appearance at the other window, high up to the right. I was horrified to see him climb out into the dark space and make his way to a bunch of stalagmites, on which he placed two or three blazing Bengal lights. Wishing to get a view from both points, I desired Nick to come back and conduct me to the upper window … I became so giddy that I was obliged to crouch down and hold on to the stalagmites. No one but the guide ever goes out to that place."[22]

Nick's adventures with the much-enthralled F. J. Stevenson continued. Stevenson had Nick accompany him and others on an exploring trip into the bottom of the Maelstrom, a very deep pit at what was considered the terminus of the cave trail in Cleaveland Avenue, near Croghan Hall. Stevenson's desire to experience the unknown had him being lowered to the bottom of the pit by rope. One can almost imagine the less than companionable thoughts that must have entered Nick's mind as he held the rope that held the English caving client. Worse still, Stevenson compelled Nick and white guide Frank Demumbrun to be lowered into the pit, as well.

Even though Nick seems to have been a reluctant participant, his trip down into the Maelstrom certainly gave him bragging rights. Yet, the few visitors' accounts that describe him state that he only pointed out the Maelstrom pit without mentioning he had been in it.

On another occasion, Stevenson had Nick take him on a boat to explore the underground cave rivers. Once in the stream, Stevenson realized the boat was, as Nick had suggested, overloaded with too many explorers. He had Nick get out and wait on a mud bank, while he and the other three occupants maneuvered the boat into the darkness. Nick did not like the idea of staying in a spot where he could not leave the cave without a boat, and he said so. Several hours later, when the boat returned, Stevenson wrote that Nick "had made up his mind that I had met with an accident and that he would be left alone to die in the darkness.... He swore he would go no more with me on voyages of discovery for love or money."[23]

For many years, park rangers have told the story that Nick Bransford bought his freedom by capturing and selling eyeless cave fish to visitors. It is upon an F. J. Stevenson first-person account that this story is based. Stevenson claimed in his reminiscences that Nick had fished in the solitude for white, eyeless cave fish in a homemade boat (perhaps the very one Nick was cast out of) on the Roaring River inside the cave. The fish were a novelty, due to their rare existence, and were easily sold for three dollars each to visitors. According to the Englishman, Nick had purchased his freedom from Thomas L. Bransford prior to Stevenson's 1863 visit.

While Nick was accompanying Stevenson on his many cave adventures, the Civil War was the primary concern above ground. In fact, a crowd of Union soldiers accompanied the group into the cave the day they descended the Maelstrom. Later that day, Mammoth Cave Hotel Proprietor E. K. Owsley celebrated the event with a "fandango" and supper that included soldiers and neighboring slaves.[24]

Tours of the cave did not cease during the war, but business was certainly hampered by a Confederate raid that occurred in December 1861. A Confederate private, Henry J. Carter, wrote his wife a letter stating that there were about 3,000 Union soldiers in the area hidden and protected by high bluffs over the Green River. He said the Confederates hoped that a raid on the Mammoth Cave Hotel would draw the Federals out into the open.[25]

Mr. Owsley received a warning that same month that Confederate General Thomas C. Hindman retreated from his position at Bell's Tavern in Barren County and meant to burn the hotel. Owsley immediately gathered the most valuable items that could be carried and hid them inside Mammoth Cave. Owsley was a Unionist, but he was also a slaveholder. He protected his "live property" by hiding them in a cave across the Green River. He locked the hotel registers, receipt accounts and business papers in an iron safe and had it rolled out into the yard. Within two days, the Confederates were there, taking everything they could use or that might be of any monetary value.[26]

"…Men helped themselves freely to choice liquors, cutlery, bedding, cooking utensil, etc…. "[27]

"They broke open the iron safe and took all the papers, registers, and accounts. Much of the furniture that they could not use was destroyed in mere wantonness."[28]

In 1863, President Abraham Lincoln issued the Emancipation Proclamation, freeing slaves in states that had seceded from the Union. This did not apply to slaves living in Kentucky, as the state had not seceded. That same year, Kentucky was exempted from Federal recruitment of African Americans, but Kentucky slaves began enlisting in Ohio, Indiana and occupied southern states.

It appears that few Edmonson County slaves sought to join the Union army, even though soldiers were in the area through much of the war. Recruiting stations existed in Glasgow, Cave City and Munfordville, none of which were far from the cave. The 12th U.S. Colored Heavy Artillery Division was stationed at Bowling Green. Yet, even with Union forces billeted at the hotel, slaves at Mammoth Cave seemed to be uninterested in volunteering.[29] Of the six black veterans living in Edmonson County between 1870 and 1910, none were residents of the county when they joined.[30]

One of those six veterans was William Garvin, who mustered in as a private in the 108th U.S. Colored Infantry at Bowling Green on February 7, 1865. Garvin settled in Edmonson County following the war and married Nick Bransford's daughter, Hannah. William soon became a guide at Mammoth Cave. It was Will who discovered the Corkscrew passageway that became an alternate route back to the entrance from the cave's lowest regions. Will was also the first to see an illusion he called the Statue of Martha Washington, caused by lanterns carried by an oncoming group of visitors as they illuminated the limestone walls around them in the 1870s. Some credit him with the discovery of Colossal Caverns, one of many caves now protected within Mammoth Cave National Park. Will filed for and received a Civil War disability pension in August 1886. Shortly following his death, Hannah filed and received a veteran's widow pension in 1906.[31]

It was the quiet and introspective Nick who donated the land for the Mammoth Cave school where his grandchildren learned to read and write. Quiet, illiterate Nick Bransford was a spiritual man—a wise man who knew what mattered most. Of the three slaves who came to Mammoth Cave in 1838, it was Nick who lived longest. He died in 1895, after having been "retired" from cave guiding due to declining health. Nick left behind daughters Hannah Garvin and Annie Brown and their children. His grave site is unknown, but it may be at the large Pleasant Union Baptist Church Cemetery near Three Springs, just off Flint Ridge Road in Mammoth Cave National Park.

I walked behind a tour group of vacationing visitors, while my partner led them to the next stop at the Snowball Room. As is the custom, I answered questions and offered guidance, while I made my way through the room, directing visitors to restrooms and benches. In my usual manner I subconsciously scanned the walls of the elliptically shaped room as I escorted the slower walkers in the group. Names and dates from the 19th century are easily read on many walls of Mammoth Cave, but hundreds are indiscernible. No one had seen this gypsum-encrusted room until Stephen Bishop's first Echo River crossing 150 years before.

What is that? Is that black lettering trying to weave its way through a familiar patch of soot? I switched on my flashlight and moved it to a different angle, first left, then right. Yes. Yes, it *is* handwriting. It looks like charcoal pencil ... let me see if I can ... yes, there it is! How did I miss this before? Does anyone else know it's here?

> "TO NICK, THE GUIDE
> AUGUST 17, 1857"

Nick was here. The summer Stephen died, Nick Bransford led visitors into this mineral-encrusted underground room, miles from the entrance of Mammoth Cave. He was the guide, their slave guide. And they honored him in stone.

The Bransford Legacy

Stephen Bishop was the most praised of the slave guides, and Nicholas Bransford lived into the 1890s. But it was Materson Bransford's cave guiding legacy that survived, unbroken, for more than a century. Mat Bransford spent many hours in the cave with Stephen Bishop, yet his name is rarely mentioned regarding the more memorable cave discoveries. It seems credit for most of the early cave route expansion is given to Stephen alone, and perhaps justifiably so.

Like Nick, Mat was the property of Thomas Bransford. He, too, was purchased by the son, Thomas L. Bransford, when the elder Bransford died. The two slaves were about the same age, and each lived out their remaining years of slavery at Mammoth Cave. Each lived all their years of manumission at Mammoth Cave, as well.

While there were other similarities between the two, there was one very marked difference between them—a difference that Mat's blood relatives acknowledged. Mat was the son of his first owner, Thomas Bransford. It was Mat's half-brother who bought him, along with Nick and Nick's child, Hannah, from Thomas Bransford, Sr.'s estate.

Descendants of Thomas Bransford admit to the biracial kinship to this day. The following comes from a letter written by Thomas Bransford's great-granddaughter, Nellie, who was reminiscing about her mother, Ann L. Hayslip, Bransford's granddaughter: "Many times have I heard her speak of those times at her grandpa's. She seemed to hold their memory in perfect reverence. She visited the Mammoth Cave with her parents in 1845 and saw Mat, the boy of Great-Grandpa's."[32]

There are several photos of Mat Bransford, which all bear witness to his parentage. Mat may well have been even more fair-featured than Stephen Bishop. In some photographs, his eyes appear to be light in color. Yet, when his portrait was sketched by Danish painter Ferdinand Richardt in 1857, his eyes were rendered a soft brown, his facial features recognizably Caucasian. He wears an expression of patience and kindness that must have touched the heart of the artist. Richardt sketched Nick Bransford as well. During his visit to Mammoth Cave, the artist spent many hours underground sketching cave scenes, some of which he later used as the basis for paintings. He made at least one landscape drawing of the Mammoth Cave Hotel and yard, including the stagecoach pulled up to the door. It is interesting that Richardt sketched the two young slaves, as he rarely created portraits. He was known as a landscape painter and one of his European landscapes is displayed in the White House.

So, why the portraits of two slaves? One can only guess, but Richardt, Mat and Nick were about the same age and it would seem the artist wanted to remember them. Many years later, one of his descendants made a gift of more than a dozen of the original Mammoth Cave sketches to the National Park Service. Among them was the original Nick Bransford portrait on sketch paper. The original portrait of Mat remains in the Richardt family, and is currently lovingly guarded by Frank and Justina Keller in New Orleans, Louisiana. Mrs. Keller is the artist's granddaughter.

The lives of slaves at Mammoth Cave bore little resemblance to the more stereotypical slavery conditions of the plantation South. Kentucky did not have a long growing season like many of the more southerly states. The most productive agricultural land was near Lexington, Bardstown, Frankfort and other areas in north central Kentucky or along the Ohio River. Farmers raised crops like tobacco, hemp and grain. Growing and harvesting these crops was not nearly as labor intensive as the work required to harvest the rice, sugar cane or cotton of the Deep South. Of course, just like in the movies, every Kentucky slave knew what it meant to be "sold down river." They understood that being taken further south would likely result in a much harder way of life, with a longer growing season, exposure to diseases and a harsher, hot climate.

As previously mentioned, when farmers had their crops in for the year, it was common for them to lease slaves to merchants or industry until planting time came around again. Many of the slave owners in Kentucky owned only house servants. Of course, on larger agricultural farms there was a slave caste system somewhat similar to the caste system of large plantations. The closer you were to the owner's family, the higher you were in the social system. House servants were considered to be at the highest level of importance, followed by blacksmiths, gardeners and stable keepers. That left field hands as lowest class, but there were typically more of them.

"House slaves had an enormous cultural impact on both the slave community and the white family because they were exposed to and carried both cultures. House slaves adopted white speech patterns, ate better food, had better clothes, and had a changing variety of work."[33]

Almost all slaves at Mammoth Cave worked in the immediate area of the cave hotel where there was daily interaction with managers and guests. There were very few slaves maintained at the cave year round, but during heavy months of visitation—typically May through September—a rather large number of slaves had to be leased from farmers and other slave owners to maintain high services at the Mammoth Cave Hotel. Proprietors needed chamber maids, cooks and handymen. There was often a need for a few more guides. For instance one slave, Jonathan Doyle, spent summers guiding cave tours for various Mammoth Cave lessees, first as a slave and later as a freed man.

Mat Bransford and other Mammoth Cave servants were more exposed to the ways of the world than were many white men of their day. They saw the latest fashions and heard the latest world news. They were present during political discussions and heard about new ways to prepare food in the East. They were also, to be sure, far more aware of arguments being raised about slavery than many other slaves or even slave owners.

Because Mammoth Cave attracted an elite class from both the United States and abroad, it is fair to assume that Mat was sometimes questioned about his personal views. While leading cave tours, the guide's race and place in society often took a backseat to the uniqueness of the cave and the jocularity and companionship of the experience at hand. In the cave, visitors sometimes interacted with the guides to a more expanded degree than they would in the hotel dining room.

In Kentucky, slaves could marry other slaves, although the marital bond could be severed at any time should one of them be sold. Freed slaves were allowed to marry other freed slaves, but they could not marry slaves. Mat Bransford was married to Parthena, a woman who was owned by a slaveholder with a farm located two miles from Mammoth Cave. His wife's owner let them live together on his land, and Mat saved enough money to build a small home for his family. At least four children were born to them in slavery.

While many abolitionists visited the cave, even they often held to preconceived notions and racial stereotypes about slaves. Despite Mat's connection to the affluent Thomas L. Bransford and his sister Mary Jane Eubanks, he could do nothing to stop his wife's owner from selling three of their children.[34] One visitor, an abolitionist named Rusling, assumed the loss of those three children had no real impact on Mat. "I don't suppose you missed these children much? You colored people never do, they say." Mat wasted no time telling him otherwise.[35]

Thomas L. Bransford never took Mat away from his situation at Mammoth Cave. Perhaps he felt his half-brother was in the best situation he could be, given that his station was that of a slave. Or maybe, despite the fact that at least two of Mat's relatives acknowledged his kinship privately, they were not quite ready to do so in Glasgow or Nashville where they and their families resided. Thomas L. Bransford served as president of the Nashville and Cincinnati Railroad Company and was Tennessee's Whig candidate for Congress in 1843. He was a successful merchant with holdings in both Tennessee and Kentucky.

There has been no documentation uncovered that bears witness to Mat Bransford ever receiving his freedom prior to 1865. Mat was allowed to see a little of the world, however. When he traveled to Louisville in 1863 during the war, his presence in the city warranted a piece in the local newspaper, the *Louisville Daily Journal:* "No one who has visited Mammoth Cave during the last quarter of a century has forgotten Mat, the colored guide, to whose attentions they have been indebted for most of their pleasurable remembrances of a visit to that great subterranean wonder.... He is familiar with the geographical and chemical formations peculiar to the Cave, and discourses of all its wonders with an apparent knowledge of his subjects that would do credit to Professor Silliman. Mat arrived in this city yesterday and is a guest of our friends of the Louisville Hotel. He will sit for his portrait today at Brown's daguerrean saloon, after which he will take a shy at whatever is worth looking at above ground hereabout, returning to the Cave tomorrow."[36]

The Civil War ended and freed slaves in Edmonson County had a choice to make. Leave or stay? Most stayed. Mammoth Cave researcher Jeanne C. Schmitzer makes these observations: Unlike much of Kentucky and the rest of the South, records give no indication of whites unwilling to sell to blacks in Edmonson County.[37] Between 1866 and 1876 there was a rapid progression of land purchases by black residents. By 1880 there were eighty black property owners in Edmonson County—14.5 percent of the county's entire black population. Thirty were in the immediate vicinity of Mammoth Cave.[38]

While they planted mainly tobacco and corn, some diversified into fruit, sheep and other products. Jesse Jeralds planted two enormous orchards, one of peaches and the other apples. Martha Lively, widow of veteran Henry Lively, enhanced her pension earnings by raising bees to produce honey and wax.[39] The number of black landowners in Edmonson County remained high compared to surrounding counties with greater black populations well into the 20th century. In 1920, 14 percent of Edmonson County's black population continued to hold property compared to slightly over six percent in Hart County, and two percent in Warren County, each of which had significantly higher black populations.

On December 5, 1870, Mat married Parthena Coats "in the road in Barren County," as witnessed by Nancy and R. T. Brown.[40] The author does not yet know if Parthena had been Mat's wife prior to that date. It is possible that they were legally proclaiming their marriage, as freed slaves were encouraged to do following the war. The 1880 Edmonson County Census describes the household (see top of page 53).

Looking to census records for family history can sometimes be confusing, providing more questions than answers. If one were to take the census on the next page as the absolute truth, one would have to believe that Mat Bransford was eight years old when he became a Mammoth Cave guide. It is more likely that Mat was 60 years old in 1880. Taken as written, Parthena would have been 12 years of age when daughter Josephine was born. That is possible, but we hope it is unlikely.

Name	Relation	Marital Status	Gender	Race	Age	Birth	Occupation
Mat BRANSFORD	Self	M	M	MU	50	KY	Guide in M. Cave
Parthena BRANSFORD	Wife	M	F	MU	45	KY	Keeping House
Josephine BRANSFORD	Daughter	D	F	MU	33	KY	
Thomas BRANSFORD	Son	S	M	MU	25	KY	
William BRANSFORD	Son	S	M	MU	14	KY	Works on Farm
Henry BRANSFORD	Son	S	M	MU	13	KY	Works on Farm
James BRANSFORD	Son	S	M	W	11	KY	
Lovel LEE	Other	S	M	W	7	KY	

Another possibility is that Parthena may not be Josephine's natural mother.

Thomas Bransford, the oldest son, does not seem to work anywhere, yet the two younger boys, William and Henry, do work. What the census record does not tell the researcher is that both William and Henry are actually Mat's grandsons. They were each fathered by a white neighbor, who shall remain unidentified here. It is also possible that Josephine and Thomas are two children who were sold away from Mat and their mother and traveled back home to their parents when freedom came.

James Bransford and Lovel Lee are cited as being sons, but they could be grandsons. Their race is listed as "white." This could possibly be a census taker's mistake. Biracial children were normally described as mulatto. Children born to unmarried mothers are often listed as "other," "lodger" or "boarder" on early census records. It is obvious, however, that this Bransford family bore more genetic ties to white ancestors than to black.

There is another son of Mat Bransford who is not listed with his father's household, because he had a household of his own in 1880. He was an older Henry Bransford, born in 1849, who was a farmer and a Mammoth Cave guide. He and his wife Alice are shown as the parents of six children. The parents and children are all described as mulatto. The eldest is 10-year-old daughter Mary Jane (named after Mat's sister?) followed by Lizzie, 8; Charles, 6; Louis, 4; John Henry, 2; and Matthew, one month. A male boarder, Ed Hawkins, also mulatto and listed as 21 years of age, is identified as a member of the household. No occupation is given.

Henry Bransford represented the second generation of Bransford guides at Mammoth Cave, guiding tours as early as 1872. The exact number of years he spent as a cave guide is unknown, but at least one visitor wrote that Henry accompanied his father on their cave tour, carrying the meal basket at the back of the group. A German visitor who described Henry as being "world famous" wrote this of Bransford: "Our guide (Henry) is a handsome young Negro man built like Hercules, tall and broad-shouldered. On Echo River, he sang with a full melodious voice … then gave out a three-tone sequence of notes, which came back a splendid chord."[41]

Visitor Adam Binkerd referred to him as the "inimitable Henry," and described him as the walking "thesaurus of the cave." He also said the young man had "an ample supply of witty sayings and irresistible drollery, coupled with the dry humor of his father."

Mammoth Cave researcher Harold Meloy described another of the visitor accounts: "Henry delighted in showing the saltpeter hoppers used during the War of 1812 and the road through the main cave along which ox carts brought petre dirt to the hoppers. Tracks of the cart wheels remained in the road as did some of the corncobs at the place where the oxen had been tethered and fed. One visitor observed that the cobs appeared perfectly preserved by the pure cave air and asked to purchase one as a keepsake. Henry obliged, and then said that he would carry in more cobs for future visitors."[42]

A watercolor portrait of Henry Bransford hung on his son Charlie's wall for many years. The youngest generation of Bransford guides, Henry's grandsons, remembered seeing it there when they visited their uncle in Glasgow following the establishment of Mammoth Cave National Park. None of the family interviewed by the author knows the location of the watercolor painting, but a photographed copy of it is safeguarded at Mammoth Cave National Park. Charlie, the eldest of Henry and Alice's sons, was kind enough to allow National Park Service staff to photograph the painting while it was in his possession.

Mat Bransford, the freed slave, died in 1886. His son, Henry, also a freed slave, died only eight years later. Just months before he left this world, Henry sat with the rest of the family to hear his nephew, William Bransford, tell stories about the big city of Chicago, Illinois. Eighteen years Henry's junior, Will was also a cave guide. He joined the guide force in 1888 and was selected to represent Mammoth Cave at the 1893 World's Fair in Chicago. The theme of the fair was "White City" and many pounds of sparkling white gypsum from Cleaveland Avenue in Mammoth Cave accompanied Will.

William Bransford was tall and lean. His complexion was fair and his hair and beard were straight, with just the slightest hint of curl. Some historians have made the conjecture that Will was selected for the Chicago trip because his Caucasian features might serve him well in a big city. William represented Mammoth Cave and Kentucky beautifully. Prior to making the journey, he and other guides were told to go to an area near the Snowball Room to collect gypsum specimens.

Gypsum is a lovely white mineral and forms readily on walls in dry areas of the cave. It was one of the primary minerals removed from the cave by prehistoric explorers. To the knowledge of Mammoth Cave historians, no prehistoric explorers ever crossed the cave's underground streams, so the gypsum-laden areas Stephen Bishop found were pristine. He was so taken by the beauty of the sparkling mineral that he named one heavily encrusted area "Charlotte's Grotto," to honor his young wife.

The large gypsum flowers, snowballs, nodules and crusts collected in 1893 were broken into small pieces and placed in small brown paper envelopes imprinted with the Mammoth Cave name and identifying the contents as gypsum. The souvenirs were distributed to hundreds, if not thousands, of fair-goers. Undoubtedly, William's attendance at the fair and the mass distribution of gypsum were marketing attempts to draw more visitors to the cave.

Following the 1893 World's Fair, the cave passageway, now partially stripped of the beautiful, sparkling minerals it had displayed through 50 years of tours and three generations of Bransford guides, became known as "Specimen Avenue." The name continues today.

By 1917 Will Bransford was head guide at Mammoth Cave, an honor bestowed upon him due to his seniority and credibility with the other guides. As late as 1923, Will continued to be responsible for distributing wages to both seasonal and year-round guides. The long-term guides for at least some of those years included Will, Josh Wilson, Louis Bransford, Elzie Bransford, Frank Berry, John Nelson and Matt Bransford. Four of the guides were black; Josh Wilson, John Nelson and Frank Berry (also spelled "Barry") were white.

Beginning in 1908, young German cartographer Max Kaemper spent one year of his life working beside an older black man as they explored and mapped Mammoth Cave. In 1917, the year the United States declared war against Germany, Max's companion (and Will's friendly competition) left the cave region, having spent 31 of his 51 years as a guide at Mammoth Cave. His name was Ed Bishop, and he claimed to be kin to Stephen.

Sitting cross-legged on the carpeted floor of my neighbors' home in Park City, I looked through box after box of treasures. It was the mid-1990s, and I was visiting with Jim and Betty Bell. Jim had been a seasonal cave guide "way back" and Betty was the daughter of Cecil Cutliff, a cave guide turned park ranger in 1941. Betty's face was illuminated, recalling stories of people she had loved and the childhood she remembered. I poured over Cecil's letters of commendation, old pay stubs, cave brochures and photos as both Jim and Betty dropped documents and scraps of paper into my lap so fast I couldn't keep up. A small, square book landed on my leg and Betty said, "I don't know where this came from. It belongs to a Josie, and we have a Josie, but it wasn't hers."

I picked up the dainty little book with its cover illustration of Mammoth Cave's entrance. It was an autograph book, painstakingly signed by a circle of friends and family in the early 1890s. The pages held several short Victorian verses, simple remembrances and numerous signatures. Here's one from Eddie, declaring that she should have a wonderful life with the wine of flowers as sweet as she. Here is another page where Eddie signed, and he signed the last page of the book, too. Some of the verses are addressed to Josie.... "Betty," I said, "do you know what you have? You have an autograph book that belonged to Josie Curd, a young black girl from Cave City." And Eddie, well ... Ed Bishop would shortly be her husband. He was courting her in an autograph book!

There's No Place Like Home

Ed Bishop began his guiding career in 1886. He, like Will Bransford, was born in 1866, one year after manumission. Ed Bishop's childhood was like that of many children in the years immediately following slavery. His mother, Louvenia Bishop, and his grandfather, Tandy Bishop, raised him. All are identified on Kentucky's 1870 Metcalfe County census when Eddie was four years old. His sister, Gabriella, was a toddler and his older brother, Schuyler, lived and worked on the farm next door as a laborer. Theirs is an extended matrilineal family, with a single mother and her children living with her father.[43]

In 1873, Eddie's mother married George Davidson in Glasgow Junction (Park City). David and Julie Bishop, who had legally declared their own 30-year marriage in 1870, witnessed the union. It is possible that the surname is coincidental and David and Julie were friends or family of George Davidson. Perhaps David and Tandy had been slaves of someone named Bishop and retained that surname after manumission. The Marriage Bond identifies George W. Davidson as principal, and Tandy Bishop as surety.[44] It is documented that David Bishop was born in Kentucky about 1810, and both his parents were born in Virginia. David Bishop's role in the lives of Louvenia and Tandy is unknown as of this writing, but will continue to be researched.

By 1880, Ed Bishop was 14 years old and living in Cave City with Hugh and Hester Shobe and their children. Ed was a laborer for the Shobes, one of many black families farming in Barren County. The Curd family lived about 10 houses away.[45]

In 1886, Ed Bishop began his guiding career at Mammoth Cave, as his signatures on cave walls attest. Visitors also mention Ed in letters and published travel articles. Many identify Ed as a descendant of Stephen Bishop. Some identify him as a son, others as a grandson. The most persistent claim is that Ed is Stephen's grandnephew. This is very hard to prove, but reasonable conjectures can be made. Franklin Gorin claimed to own both Stephen's mother and his brother, after the boys had been born. It is very possible that Tandy Bishop was Stephen's brother and Louvenia his niece. This kinship would, indeed, make Ed the grandnephew of Stephen Bishop. To date, it remains an unproven, but plausible theory.

Guide Will Bransford made his trip to Chicago in 1893, the same year

Ed Bishop married Josie Curd of Barren County.[46] Their marriage lasted only a few years, during which they lost an infant daughter, Chancie. The marriage ended with Josie's death from tuberculosis. A portrait of Josie Curd is in the possession of her niece, Elnora Harriford, in Smith's Grove, Kentucky.

Ed's second marriage, to Miss Willie Lewis, occurred in March 1900.[47] They had four children, Stephen, Maude, Tandy and Anna. In 1909, their father named four of his new Mammoth Cave discoveries—Stephen's Way, Maud's Grotto, Tan's Pit and Runt's Dome—after his two sons and two daughters.

Ed Bishop was a stocky, handsome man, described as mulatto on all census records. He was a strong caver and spent many hours underground with Will Bransford, Ed Hawkins, William Garvin and the other "exploring" guides. By the time this Bishop came to the cave, old Mat Bransford was gone, but his great-grandson, Matt, would soon join the guide force. Nick Bransford was around for the first few years Ed was at the cave, and he would certainly have heard many stories from the old cave fish salesman.

When German cartographer Max Kaemper arrived at Mammoth Cave after a visit in the eastern states, he came as any other visitor. He quickly became enthralled with the underground labyrinth and arranged with the cave manager, Henry Ganter, to receive room and board in exchange for creating a detailed map of the cave. Ed Bishop, about 15 years Max's senior, became Kaemper's caving partner and their story is a major one in Mammoth Cave exploration history.

Ed Bishop and Max Kaemper made many new discoveries in the cave, substantially increasing the number of known miles of passageways. Their frequent caving expeditions resulted in more known cave beyond the furthest point in Broadway Avenue. That spot was celebrated by Stephen Bishop nearly seven decades earlier when he climbed up a mound of collapsed limestone layers to lay on his back and scrawl his name on an exposed layer of limestone at the ceiling. It was under and around that miserable wall that the latter Bishop and Kaemper went on to find Kaemper Hall, Bishop Pit, Elisabeth's Dome and Violet City.

As the fourth generation of Bransfords joined the guide force, they found themselves working side-by-side with white guides like John Nelson and Schuyler Hunt. They also walked back and forth to work with each other. "Residential segregation in the Mammoth Cave community was non-existent, and families shared equal economic status. As rural subsistence farmers, black and white neighbors depended on each other's assistance during planting and harvest, childbearing, family illness and for fellowship."[48] When Shelvy Bransford became extremely ill, white neighbors stayed at his home to support and help his parents until he recovered.[49]

Clifton Bransford, son of Mammoth Cave guide Louis Bransford, described the interaction between the white and black neighbors. On warm nights in summer, white guides Josh Wilson and Frank Berry might bring their families over to see Louis and Matt Bransford and their families at home, and vice-versa. They drank coffee, talked about whatever came to mind and chewed tobacco, while the children played outside. As Clifton told me and a group of friends during a visit with him in Indiana, "Every night we'd get together with the Frank Berrys. Either they'd come to our house or we'd go down there. It was just wonderful."[50]

His cousin, David Bransford, spoke about the familiar ties between each of the families along the adjoining country roads. "When we moved away from there (Mammoth Cave) we found out it was quite a bit different."[51]

While the guide force had been primarily black since 1838, white guides began to seek jobs at the cave around the turn of the 20th century. Before the Civil War, the Mammoth Cave estate was fairly self-contained, only supplementing the year-round servants with seasonal help from outside. Following the war, many of the blacks stayed in the immediate vicinity of the estate, making it easy to walk or ride a horse to the hotel in a reasonable amount of time. In 1830, 25 percent of Kentucky's population was black. By 1900, the black population had dropped to 13 percent. As black families in Edmonson County decided to leave the area and move north for jobs, white families bought the property and settled in. The railroad and automobiles also made transportation to and from the cave less time consuming. Although new modes of transportation over the ridges and valleys presented their own challenges, managers at Mammoth Cave were no longer so dependent on the hired help that lived nearby.

Of all the Mammoth Cave occupations, that of cave guide was the most integrated and unified job. When many of the white guides were hired, black predecessors and coworkers trained them. The job required significant teamwork and, consequently, a close fellowship developed between guides regardless of color.[52]

The Mammoth Cave Hotel staff and the guide force worked in a unique situation for its time. "Blacks and whites worked together in building and grounds maintenance, and trail and bridge maintenance inside the cave. On the other hand, only blacks worked as porters and waiters, and only whites worked as clerks and managers. Accordingly, certain demands would only be made of a black employee. For example, black employee Ed Hawkins had to cancel his participation in a planned cave exploration because one of the managers needed him to peel potatoes…. There is little doubt that his abilities would have been better utilized had he participated in the exploring expedition."[53]

Ed Hawkins is listed on various Edmonson County census records from 1880 until 1930, and each decade he appears to be living in a different household. In 1907, he and Will Bransford, along with New Yorker Benjamin F. Einbigler, discovered Cathedral Domes, an impressive series of vertical shafts. "Bransford Avenue" and "Hawkins' Way" were named after the two guides.[54]

The Mammoth Cave community survived the best way they could, tilling soil that sat in the bottom of sinkholes. Numerous families made extra money working at the cave, serving as laundresses, porters, drivers, waiters, cooks and maids. Men like Old Jim Brown[55] and Ed Hawkins worked odd jobs for the estate, making small structural repairs, chopping wood and plucking chickens—whatever needed to be done.

Oral tradition conveys that Hawkins' hands were so big he could take the feathers off a chicken in only two swipes. Photographs of Ed Hawkins are recognizable, as he always wore large blanket pins to pull together the front of his shirt or jacket. Perhaps his hands and fingers were so large they made manipulating small shirt buttons a chore and he replaced them with the blanket pins. Sadly, Ed Hawkins died at Western State Hospital in Hopkinsville, Kentucky, having been a patient there for more than five years. His 1936 death was attributed to chronic myocarditis, with a contributing factor of senility. He is buried in the hospital cemetery.[56]

The year 1917 was a turning point for the Mammoth Cave estate. The hotel burned to the ground in December 1916 and a number of changes were taking place. An incidental meeting of a chapter of the Ku Klux Klan had been held at the cave hotel in 1916. The Mammoth Cave heirs (the Croghan influence was still at hand) had placed a woman, Donna Bullock, in charge of business matters. She, in turn, regularly communicated with Judge Albert C. Janin, husband of Mammoth Cave heir Violet Blair Janin.

Various letters between Ms. Bullock and Janin describe complaints from the guides. At one point, when Will Bransford came to Ms. Bullock to voice the guides' concerns that management was taking advantage of them, she told him that if the guides did not like the way things were being run they could leave, and she would find other guides. She informed Judge Janin in a daily report that Will simply laughed and told her that guiding tours in Mammoth Cave was a job no one else wanted to do.

"The team unity that developed among guides afforded them some degree of power in work conditions. In 1917, they complained to manager Donna Bullock about their grueling work schedule, and proposed another plan. They forwarded a copy of their complaint and proposal to Trustee Albert C. Janin along with an appeal for a 'fair deal' in the matter. 'We are appealing to you for protection. We have certainly worked hard to try and please Miss Donna and … she has no mercy on us….' Nearly a year later the guides complained again to Bullock; this time because they were leading additional tours yet receiving no extra pay. In September they presented the matter to Trustee Janin along with documentation of extra trips. Between July and August they had led sixty-one additional tours with no compensation. Of the six guides who complained, four were black and two were white. Their cooperation as an integrated body was especially remarkable. The fact that black employees felt they could complain to their white superior was extremely unusual."[57] As a result of the group's complaint, Trustee Janin compensated the guides for their extra tours.

Ed Bishop married a third time in 1913, this time to Dora English of Louisville. In 1917, he sold his property near Salts Cave and headed north to Illinois. Had he continued his guiding career at Mammoth Cave, he might have given Will Bransford competition for the role of lead guide. But, after guiding for 31 years, he left Mammoth Cave. The Old Mammoth Cave Hotel had burned to the ground in a December fire only months before. Ed took his family north to Rock Island, Illinois, then on to Indianapolis, Indiana, where he found a home on Calvin Street. Ed spent the last years of his life working for the housekeeping department in the Indianapolis City Building. Each of his four children lived with him at various times over the years. Oldest son Stephen and his wife, Melissa, moved on to LaPorte, Indiana, where Stephen died in 1983. Ed Bishop died on June 17, 1931. He was not buried in Indianapolis, but returned to Kentucky. He rests in an unmarked grave alongside his first wife, Josie, under a large cedar tree in the Curd family cemetery located between Cave City and Glasgow, Kentucky.

Through the 1920s and 30s, numerous black guides continued to work at Mammoth Cave. Guide Matt Bransford and his wife, Zemmie, prepared meals for black cave visitors and served them at their home near Great Onyx Cave. They also provided lodging for black visitors.

Other guides turned to various labors in an effort to supplement their cave guiding income. In 1930, there were eight "fourth generation" Bransfords on the guide roster, including Clifton, Arthur, Eddie, Elzie and George. Matt Bransford, his cousin William Bransford (now called "Old Man Will") and Louis Bransford were also still working as guides. Other black guides included Bob Lively, John "Mutch" Hunter and Louis Brown.

The 1930s brought many changes for everyone in the vicinity of Mammoth Cave. Movers and shakers within Kentucky began a movement to create a national park in the state. With the 1929 death of the last heir to the Mammoth Cave estate, the Mammoth Cave National Park Association purchased the property—it did not go to auction. In continuing efforts to achieve the national park goal, hundreds of farms and homes—thousands of acres of hillsides, woods and valleys—were purchased, piece-by-piece, over a period of nearly 15 years.

Many of the younger guides, black and white, joined the Civilian Conservation Corps (CCC) to make better money during the Depression years. One of the four CCC camps at Mammoth Cave consisted of all black enrollees. One of their primary duties was to improve tour trails inside Mammoth Cave. As they worked, they greatly changed the cave floor—a dirt and stone path that had borne the feet of dozens of slaves, freed slaves and their descendants for a full century.

In 1939, Louis Bransford—the grandson of Mat Bransford—was the last of the black guides. He retired that year. When the first park rangers were sworn in two years later, they were all Caucasian. The day Louis Bransford walked to the office and turned in his key to the iron door guarding Mammoth Cave's entrance marked the end of 101 continuous years of Bransford guides at Mammoth Cave. His departure did not symbolize the end of an era, but the end of a way of life.

When it was all said and done, families who lived and worked together for generations found themselves packing their belongings and leaving behind their homes, their churches, their schools, their jobs and their cave. Race did not seem to matter much as they left and went their separate ways. Race would matter a great deal as the black families confronted new realities in unfamiliar surroundings. They could not buy or rent a home just anywhere they pleased. There was no longer a white neighbor like Martin Shackleford or Josh Wilson willing to sell them some land, co-sign a note or, if necessary, show them where to sign or make their mark on legal documents. Only certain streets in Cave City allowed "colored." Only certain sections of Louisville allowed "colored." Only specific streets in Detroit or Indianapolis allowed "colored." Blacks realized they might as well rent in the city since few would sell to them in the country. Many didn't want to live next door to "colored."

Extended families tried to live within walking distance of each other. But, as children married, they began to scatter to large cities to find jobs. After only two generations away from Mammoth Cave, their youngest children did not know about Old Man Will who went to Chicago, Ed Hawkins and his blanket pins or Uncle Jim Brown who had been a slave in Louisville. They did not know the thrill of crawling into a sparkling room encrusted with gypsum, knowing you were leaving the first marks ever left by human hands in the soft, unbroken surface of dust on the cave floor. For years, their heritage was almost lost and they had no idea where they could find it. Now they do.

Clifton Bransford died in 1996, only a couple of years after I met with him for three hours in his small, hot, upstairs apartment in Indianapolis. Nearly 90 years old, he showed our small group how he "rolled a torch" from an old rag when he was a young cave guide—he used his handkerchief for the demonstration. He talked about how the rolled torches were dipped in kerosene and thrown from a torch stick, off into the dark corners of the cave to light up walls and ceilings. He laughed when we showed him photographs and he recognized Josh Wilson, a smile further lighting an already illuminated face as he chortled, "Well, there's old Josh … I sure never thought I'd see old Josh, again…." He talked about how his father, Louis Bransford, and Louis' cousin, Will, had a permanent game of checkers set up inside the old guide house, and everyone knew better than to touch that checkerboard when they had a game in progress. He told us that Will usually won. He said he didn't see family near enough and wanted us to tell his cousin David down in Glasgow he said "Hey" and hoped he was well.

David Bransford, son of John Henry Bransford, grandson of slave guide Henry Bransford, great-grandson of slave Mat Bransford was 88 years old when he left this world in May 2003. But his children know where they can go to find peace when they need it. They know where their people first made their mark in this country. They can go home to the cave, the Mammoth Cave of Kentucky.

And, the cave will know them.

Epilogue

*O*ur small group of four moves across the Bridge of Sighs at Bottomless Pit and, lighting our lanterns, we quietly make our way into Pensico Avenue inside Mammoth Cave. I make no comment as the three young, excited new guides discover and read aloud signatures smoked and scratched on the walls, note sparkling minerals they never saw before and try to decipher the geology of the passageway. After three months, they have seen other signatures, other gypsum. They read Arthur Palmer's book on Mammoth Cave geology and know just enough about hydrology to be dangerous. The cave is no longer strange and frightening. Now they aren't so scared and nervous. The geology talk is becoming more solid. The names and history are more familiar.

They wanted to see Pensico Avenue, since they had never been there and visitors asked about it all the time. I agreed to let them visit the next day before the visitor center closed and promised them a surprise. They didn't know it, but the surprise would also be a test.

I tell them there isn't time to go far and we will turn around at "Turtle Rock." My companions are so intent upon exploring the passageway, I have to smile. I remember those feelings of discovery, of newness and oldness all mixed together. After more than two decades, I am still awed by the cave and by its people, too—the old and the new.

Turtle Rock looms ahead in the shadows of our lanterns and I lead them past it, then turn to the right to backtrack around it. The large boulder sits in the middle of the passageway, just the way time left it *when the ceiling lost its grasp and the large chunk of limestone dropped the short distance to settle on the cave floor.*

"Take a look around you; this is as far as we go," I say. "Where's the surprise?" they ask. "It's here," I say softly. "How do we find it?" they ask. "It will find you," I reply.

They put down the lanterns and start to search the rock with the strong beam of their flashlights. They pass over the cave's secret several times, enjoying the old inscriptions from cave visitors of long ago. But, the secret sits quietly, camouflaged in limestone by the hard wash of light.

I can't give this to them. The discovery needs to belong to one of them. They will need the feeling to draw from when they share the cave with others in the future … Yes, there you go, young lady, put away that flashlight and pick up that lantern. That's right.… The other two guides are now at the front of the rock, certain they have missed something there. The younger woman stands for a moment, pondering the massiveness of the rock, the solitude of the spot. Lowering the lantern, she lets soft shadows float down upon the rock, and herself.

Ah, was that a slight breath of surprise? Does she see it? Yes … yes she does. One small step forward … and the young guide slowly traces the large shape on the limestone with her finger.… It's a heart, scratched in so lightly on the rock's face, it seems meant to remain unseen by the many, only found by the few who take time to search.

There is scrawling cursive writing, like that of a child just learning … Oh, look, it's him … but she does not call to the others, not yet.

She sees the name, "Stephen Bishop, Guide of the Mammoth Cave," captured within the heart. And there she is ... "Mrs. Charlotte Bishop, the flower of the Mammoth Cave" ... his gift to her.

The young woman stands quietly for a few moments. She looks towards me, still silent. With the briefest hesitation, she extends her hand and lays it firmly upon the limestone at the center of the heart, then smiles as she feels the warm pulse of the cave.

AUTHOR'S NOTE

On April 20, 2004, Jerry Ronald Bransford worked his first day as a seasonal cave guide at Mammoth Cave National Park. Retired from a 30-year career at Dow Corning Corporation, Jerry is the son of David Bransford, the grandson of John Henry Bransford, the great-grandson of Henry Bransford and the great-great-grandson of slave guide Mat Bransford.

Kentucky African American Population Statistics, 1790 - 1940

1790 - The first U.S. census reports 73,077 persons living in Kentucky, 16 percent of them African-American slaves. Free blacks make up .2 percent of the population.

1800 - African Americans in Kentucky number 41,084, almost 19 percent of the population. Free blacks number 741, or 1.8 percent of the black population.

1810 - African Americans in Kentucky number 82,274, just over 20 percent of the population. Free blacks number 1,713, or 2.08 percent of the black population.

1820 - African Americans in Kentucky number 129,491, almost 19 percent of the population. Free blacks number 2,759, or 2.13 percent of the black population.

1830 - African Americans in Kentucky number 170,130, almost 25 percent of the population. Free blacks number 4,917, or 2.9 percent of the black population.

1840 - African Americans in Kentucky number 189,575, just over 24 percent of the population. Free blacks number 7,317, or 3.85 percent of the black population.

1850 - African Americans in Kentucky number 220,992, about 22.5 percent of the population. Free blacks number 10,011, or 4.53 percent of the black population.

1860 - African Americans in Kentucky number 236,167, almost 20.5 percent of the population. Free blacks number 10,684, or 4.52 percent of the black population.

Percentage of African Americans in total Kentucky Population 1870 - 1940:

1870	17 percent
1880	16 percent
1890	14 percent
1900	13 percent
1910	11 percent
1920	9.5 percent
1930	8 percent
1940	7.5 percent

ENDNOTES

1. *Kentucky Land Grants,* Volume 1, Part 1, Chapter IV Grants South of Green River (1797-1866); *War of 1812 Service Records,* Kentucky; *Kentucky Marriages to 1850,* Barren County.

2. Cecil E. Goode, *World Wonder Saved.* Published by the Mammoth Cave Park Association, Mammoth Cave, Kentucky, 1986.

3. Kentucky Educational Television publication, *Underground Railroad: Passage to Freedom. Kentucky African-American Timeline,* 2003.

4. Original letter in possession of Mr. J. S. Hays, Smith's Grove, Kentucky.

5. *Kentucky Marriages to 1850,* Mercer County.

6. Young George later married fellow Kentuckian Agnes Catherine Williams, became a Methodist minister and fathered five children. George died in 1886, at age 72 in Dallas, Texas. *Kentucky Marriages to 1850,* Barren County; Kentucky Census, 1850; Ancestry World Tree Project, 2003.

7. Lowry Bishop transfer of conveyance of property to Franklin Gorin, May 15, 1837, Barren County Court Clerk Records, Glasgow, Kentucky.

8. Englishman John Walker first invented matches in 1827. His "Congreve's Rockets" were the first friction matches and were made using antimony sulfide, potassium chlorate, gum and starch. A fellow named Samuel Jones saw the "Congreves" and decided to copy and sell them, calling his matches "Lucifers." They became popular, but had a bad burning odor. A French chemist, Charles Sauria, invented a match made with white phosphorous in 1830. These matches had no odor, but they caused an illness called "phossy jaw." White phosphorous is poisonous. Johan Edvard Lundstrom of Sweden finally developed a safety match in 1855 by putting red phosphorous on the sandpaper striking surface of the matchbox.

9. Alexander Clark Bullitt, *Rambles in the Mammoth Cave During the Year 1844, by a Visitor.* (New York: Johnson reprint Corporation, 1973). It is generally believed that this book, originally published in Louisville, was actually written by Dr. John Croghan in an effort to promote the cave.

10. Nathaniel Willis, *Health Trip to the Tropics,* Charles Scribner, New York, 1853.

11. Bayard Taylor, *At Home and Abroad,* G. P. Putnam, New York. Written in 1855, but published in 1864.

12. Maria Child, "Mammoth Cave," *Bentley's Miscellany* 14 (1843): 417.

13. Nathaniel Willis, Letters dated Mammoth Cave, June 1852. *The Home*

Journal, New York, August 7, 1852. *Health Trip to the Tropics.* Charles Scribner, New York. 1853.

14. Will of John Croghan, January 10, 1849, Book 4, page 181, Jefferson County Court Clerk, Louisville, Kentucky.

15. *The Stephen Bishop Story: The Man and the Legend,* 1974.

16. Inventory and Sales, December 31, 1853, Book 7, page 172, Barren County Court Clerk, Glasgow, Kentucky. A child described as "Little Hannah" was also listed in Bransford's inventory of slaves. It is probable that this was Nick Bransford's daughter, Hannah, who would have been an infant around this period of time. The identity of her mother is unknown.

17. This letter is not in the author's possession, but is the property of Ms. Pat Day, a Mary Jane Bransford descendant now living in Texas.

18. Herman Zagel, "An Excursion to Mammoth Cave in Kentucky," *Register of the Kentucky Historical Society* 71 (1973): p. 282. Account written in 1883.

19. Charles W. Wright, *A Guide Manual to Mammoth Cave* (Louisville, 1897) p. 7.

20. Author unknown, "A Tour in the Dark," *Atlantic Monthly,* December 1867, p. 670. Author's Note: Nicholas would have been no more than 40 years of age at the time of this visit.

21. Ibid. p. 677.

22. F. J. Stevenson, "Adventures Underground: the Mammoth Cave of Kentucky in 1863," *Blackwoods Magazine,* June 1932.

23. Ibid.

24. Ibid.

25. "Old Letters Tell of Damage to Mammoth Cave in Civil War," *Glasgow (KY) Daily Times,* August 17, 1931.

26. J. R. Underwood, "Report of the Affairs of the 'Mammoth Cave' for the Year 1861," April 2, 1862. Janin Family Collection, Huntington Library Manuscript Collection, San Marino, California.

27. "Old Letters Tell of Damage."

28. "Underwood, Report of Affairs ... 1861."

29. Schmitzer, Jeanne C., *The Black Experience at Mammoth Cave, Edmonson County, Kentucky 1838-1942.* Thesis. University of Central Florida. 1996. Author's Note: This is one of the best research documents written about the lives of slaves and freed men at Mammoth Cave to date.

30. Compiled service records of volunteer Union soldiers who served in organizations from the state of Kentucky. National Archives Record Group 94, Washington, D.C.

31. Civil War Pension Records, Kentucky.

32. Letter in the possession of Pat Davis, Morgan Mill, Texas. Ms. Davis is a direct descendant of Mary Jane Bransford Eubank, sister of Thomas L. Bransford and half-sister to Mat Bransford. Letter is part of a larger book of family records.

33. Genovese, Eugene D. *Roll, Jordan, Roll: The World the Slaves Made* (New York: Random House, 1972).

34. Slave families were for the most part matrilineal. Regardless of the father's identity, children were the property of their mother's owner.

35. Rusling, F., "A Trip to the Mammoth Cave of Kentucky," page 7. This is an abolitionist pamphlet in the Kentucky Historical Society Manuscript Collection, Frankfort, Kentucky.

36. *Louisville Daily Journal,* August 20, 1863.

37. Schmitzer, pages 57-58.

38. Schmitzer research, Tax Records, Edmonson County, Kentucky, 1866-1876.

39. Agricultural Schedule, Edmonson County, Kentucky, 1880. Kentucky Department of Libraries and Archives, Frankfort, Kentucky.

40. Register of Marriages, Edmonson County Court Clerk.

41. Herman Zagel, "An Excursion to Mammoth Cave," *Die Abendschule,* 1888. Translation by Richard A. Weiss in *The Register* of the Kentucky Historical Society, Frankfort, Kentucky. July, 1973, Vol. 71, No. 3, pp. 272-295.

42. Harold Meloy, "The Bransfords Show Mammoth Cave," 1983.

43. 1870 census, Metcalfe County, Kentucky. Author's Note: Metcalfe County adjoins Barren County. The community of Flat Rock, where the Bishop family lived, is very close to the county line.

44. Barren County Marriage Bond, 1873. Barren County Court Clerk.

45. 1880 census, Barren County, Kentucky.

46. Edmonson County Marriage Bond, 1893.

47. Edmonson County Marriage Bond, 1900.

48. Schmitzer, 72.

49. Clifton Bransford interview, 1992.

50. Ibid.

51. David Bransford interview, 1992.

52. Schmitzer, p. 76.

53. Ibid.

54. To the author's knowledge, Bransford Avenue is the only feature in Mammoth Cave named after any of the four generations of Bransford guides.

55. Jim Brown was listed as a slave on Dr. John Croghan's 1849 property inventory. Jim was a brother or half-brother to Charlotte Brown, wife of Stephen Bishop. The author thanks friend and researcher Norman Warnell for reminding her to look at that document again.

56. Certified Death Certificate, Kentucky, January 25, 1936. This certificate identifies Ed Hawkins' parents as Calvin Hawkins and Fannie Smith of Glasgow Junction.

57. Schmitzer, p. 77.